THE AMERICAN LANDSCAPE

I0798972

ROCKY MOUNTAINS

DWAYNE HICKS

PowerKiDS press

Published in 2026 by The Rosen Publishing Group, Inc.
2544 Clinton Street, Buffalo, NY 14224

Copyright © 2026 by The Rosen Publishing Group, Inc.

All rights reserved. No part of this book may be reproduced in any form without permission in writing from the publisher, except by a reviewer.

First Edition

Editor: Greg Roza
Book Design: Michael Flynn

Photo Credits: Cover, p. 1 Pedro Carrilho/Shutterstock.com; (series background) Omeris/Shutterstock.com; p. 5 Greg Meland/Shutterstock.com; p. 7 Rainer Lesniewski/Shutterstock.com; p. 9 stihii/Shutterstock.com; p. 11 Virrage Images/Shutterstock.com; p. 13 Cheri Alguire/Shutterstock.com; p. 15 Diane Garcia/Shutterstock.com; p. 17 Patrick Jennings/Shutterstock.com; p. 19 Alexey Kamenskiy/Shutterstock.com; p. 21 LanaG/Shutterstock.com.

Library of Congress Cataloging-in-Publication Data

Names: Hicks, Dwayne, author.
Title: Rocky Mountains / Dwayne Hicks.
Description: [Buffalo, New York] : PowerKids Press, [2025] | Series: The American landscape | Includes bibliographical references and index.
Identifiers: LCCN 2024054608 (print) | LCCN 2024054609 (ebook) | ISBN 9781499450958 (library binding) | ISBN 9781499450941 (paperback) | ISBN 9781499450965 (ebook)
Subjects: LCSH: Rocky Mountains–Juvenile literature.
Classification: LCC F721 .H54 2025 (print) | LCC F721 (ebook) | DDC 978–dc23/eng/20241203
LC record available at https://lccn.loc.gov/2024054608
LC ebook record available at https://lccn.loc.gov/2024054609

Manufactured in China

Some of the images in this book illustrate individuals who are models. The depictions do not imply actual situations or events.

CPSIA Compliance Information: Batch #QSPK26. For Further Information contact Rosen Publishing at 1-800-237-9932.

Find us on

CONTENTS

The Rockies! 4
Where in the World? 6
Rising Up 8
Weather. 10
Wildlife. 12
History of the Rockies 16
The Rocky Mountains Today. 20
Glossary 22
For More Information 23
Index 24

The Rockies!

A mountain range is a line of mountains. There are mountain ranges all over the world. The Rocky Mountains is a long mountain range in the United States and Canada. They are so big that one part of the Rockies can be very different from other parts.

Where in the World?

The Rocky Mountain range is about 3,000 miles (4,828 km) long. In some places it's more than 300 miles (483 km) wide. Some **peaks** are more than 14,000 feet (4,267 m) tall! There are many big cities in the Rockies. Denver, Colorado, is called the Mile-High City!

CANADA
Rocky Mountains
Denver
COLORADO
UNITED STATES

Rising Up

The Rocky Mountains were made by powerful forces. The top **layer** of Earth, the crust, is made up of many pieces called plates. These plates move! Over millions of years, two plates pushed into each other. This caused land to rise into the air, making the Rocky Mountains.

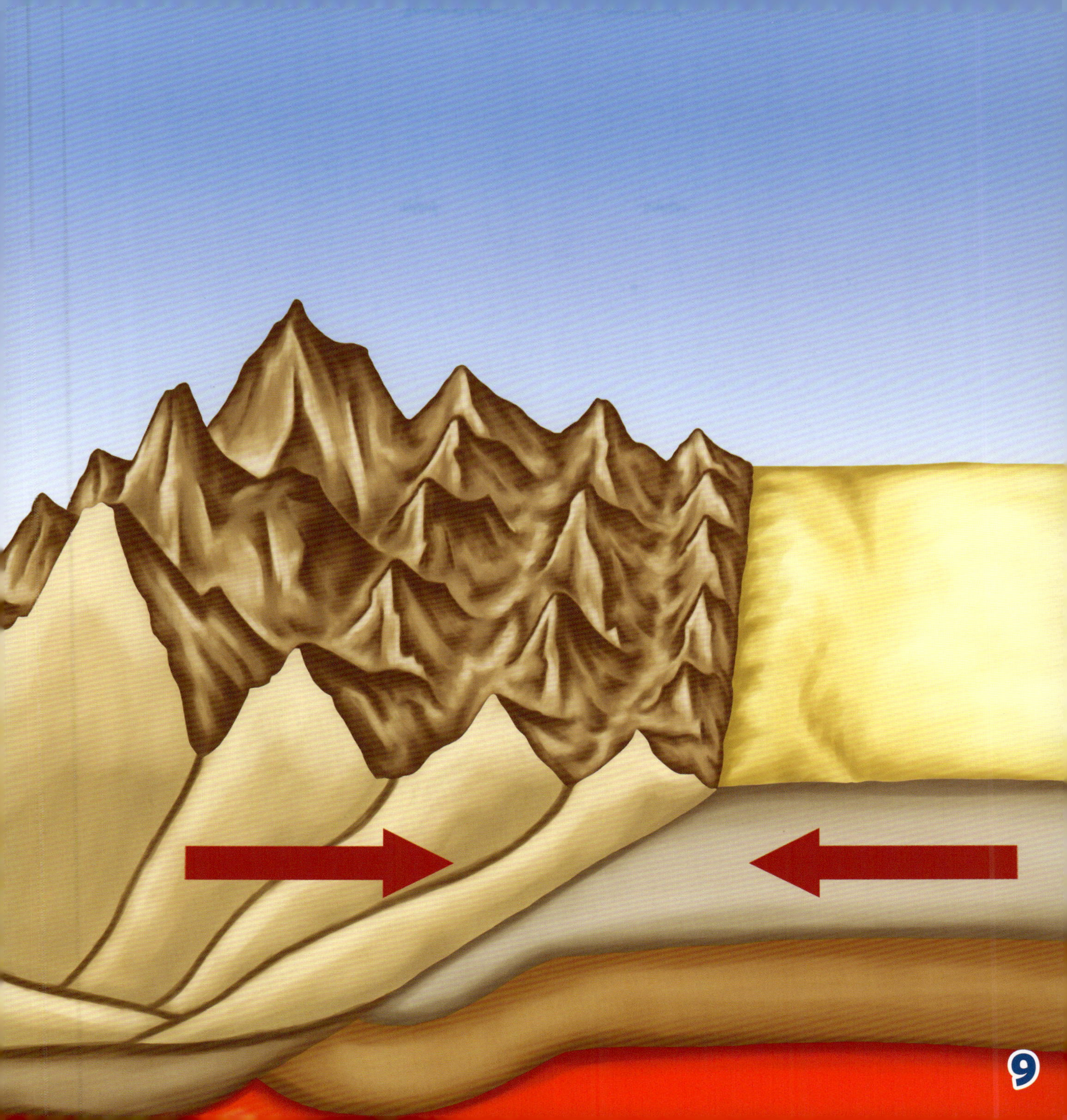

Weather

The weather of the Rocky Mountains can be very different. Many peaks are so tall they are covered with snow all year. The weather can be hot and dry at the bottom of the mountain. To the west of the mountain range, it is wet. It is drier to the east.

Wildlife

Many different plants and animals live in the Rockies—far too many to name here! This is because the Rocky Mountains cover so much land. One of the largest herds of bison live near the mountains in Wyoming. Wolves had almost disappeared from hunting, but now their numbers are growing.

Different plants and animals live at different **elevations**. Many kinds of animals live in the forests and plains at the bottom of the mountains. The higher you go, the fewer plants and animals you will see. Mountain goats climb up high in summer and go lower in winter.

Europeans first saw the Rocky Mountains in the mid-1500s. Europeans first crossed the Rockies in 1793. In the mid-1800s, hundreds of **pioneers** heading west crossed the Rockies using the Oregon Trail. Others moved to the Rockies in the hope of finding gold and silver.

The Rocky Mountains Today

Today, there are many roads, towns, and cities in and around the Rocky Mountains. People from around the world come to see the natural beauty of the Rockies every year. Some come to hike, fish, and camp. Some come to ski! Others go to national parks.

GLOSSARY

cliff: High and steep land.

culture: The beliefs and ways of life of a certain group of people.

elevation: Height above sea level.

layer: One thickness lying over or under another.

language: The words, their sounds, and the ways of combining them used and understood by a large group of people.

peak: The top of a mountain.

pioneer: One of the first people to travel to and settle in a place.

FOR MORE INFORMATION

BOOKS

Del Grande, Sarah. *A Grande Guide to Rocky Mountain National Park.* New York, NY: Overgate Press, 2024.

Gillum Lue, Julie. *What I Saw in Rocky Mountain.* Helena, MT: Riverbend Publishing, 2019.

WEBSITES

KidZone: Rocky Mountains
www.kidzone.ws/habitats/rocky-mountains.htm
Learn more about the different parts of the Rocky Mountains range, and see amazing photographs of the mountains.

Kiddle: Rocky Mountain National Park
kids.kiddle.co/Rocky_Mountain_National_Park
Read even more facts about the Rocky Mountains from this detailed website.

Publisher's note to educators and parents: Our editors have carefully reviewed these websites to ensure that they are suitable for students. Many websites change frequently, however, and we cannot guarantee that a site's future contents will continue to meet our high standards of quality and educational value. Be advised that students should be closely supervised whenever they access the internet.

INDEX

A
animals, 12, 14

B
bison, 12

D
Denver, Colorado, 6

E
elevation, 14

M
Mesa Verde National Park, 16
mountain goat, 14

N
Native Americans, 16

O
Oregon Trail, 18

P
peak, 6, 10
pioneers, 18
plants, 12, 14

S
ski, 20

W
weather, 10
wolves, 12
Wyoming, 12